SHADES OF CAREER BOOK

SABITA DAKUA

Contents

Contents

Preface

Shades of Career book is specifically created for helping youth with the guidelines about career decisions. We all are aware that at a younger age after studies we always get confused about where to start and end. Many questions get in our heads, and we may also take assistance by attending Seminars, and workshops, taking the help of elders, and even researching this topic. One thing I would like to convey is the way you are and find a source of income for a living but don't compare it. As we move ahead in life everything would be changing as per circumstances so, I have done your work a little easier by taking different field person interviews which may help you in your mindset. Hope it creates a change in the thought process.

Acknowledgements

*Milestones achieved in the journey of life are never achieved alone; this is one exception. As I completed this enlightening journey, I would like to acknowledge and thanks **Mayuresh Kallani and Naseha** put my best foot forward and making this story successful. So, first I would like to thank **6Hues Publication** who has given me this opportunity to do this project in this curriculum.*

I would also like to thank my parents, family, colleagues, and friends who inspired me to work well on the topic and see to it that the book is up to the mark.

I would also like to thank and express my gratitude to all the people who have directly and indirectly helped me in completing this book and have always been blessed with these experiences.

Disclaimer

Shades of Career book is written of real work role of common people who is ahead in career and this is for reading purposes only. Do not repeat the same things in real life as there are certain roles beyond our circumstances. Each and every person differs vary from birth to death in a new challenge so, it may happen few things will match from characters but don't assume it will end the same. This book is not to hurt any sentiments and solely responsible for their individual story itself. It is a nonfictional book and characters are solely important from the concepts. No part of this book may be reproduced in any form or by any electronic or mechanical means without written permission from the author, except for the use of brief quotations in a book review.

The Content presented in the book is collected by the author, The publishers have tried there best to make it error free & palgarised free Content. In case if there is any palgarized found solely the author is responsible, publisher should not be blamed in case..

About The Author

Sabita Dakua resides in Mumbai, Maharashtra. She has completed a master's in business administration. She is pursuing her psychology studies and compiled 4books, 2Solo books, and participated in 70+ books as co-author. She is highly motivated with many multi-skills and still seeking knowledge to groom herself. She likes to visit new places, write, read, sing, learn languages, and design clothes & foodies in her free time. In spite of their busy schedule, she likes to spend little time with friends and try to motivate them in life.

For more learning writeups follow –
*Insta Id- @words_clubbed_*
*Facebook-@sabzzwrites_*
Website-@sabitadakua.com
Blog- https://scriptiv.blogspot.com/?m=1

CHAPTER ONE

Basic Diagram of Career

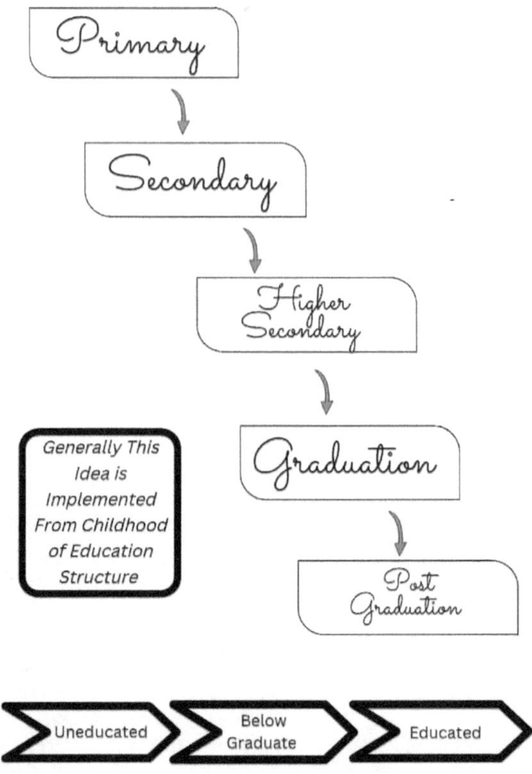

Explanation of above diagram as below-

The hierarchy from primary to postgraduate is a very logical concept for all and easily understandable. Because we always studied our rankings from the primary school itself. This may stick as a barrier if we relocate and restart in another pattern. From childhood, we learned to understand basics than solve tough questions as per our IQ.

That's fine if we do it in the same manner and move ahead in our careers. But it is nowhere written if you drop any slab of this hierarchy, you can't move ahead in your career.

For instance, a career can also be established by Cobbler, Barber, Fashion Designer, Artist, Dancer, Singer, Sole proprietor, Businessman, Contractor, Carpenter, Actor, Gardener, Writer, etc. Do they need any slab if they have talent???

Yes, your thoughts are right now we don't need a specific plan for a career. So, my suggestion is if you have one life, and you want the best please work hard with your passion. One bad decision can ruin your peace and create unhappiness in circumstances. Each person has different goals and not necessary it will be established in the same pattern might be something new is waiting for you. So, please don't compare with anyone as everyone has different qualifications but is placed in other positions. I have a few examples in real as a person interviewed for this concept. Hope this will help in understanding better.

Career Structure As Below In Reality

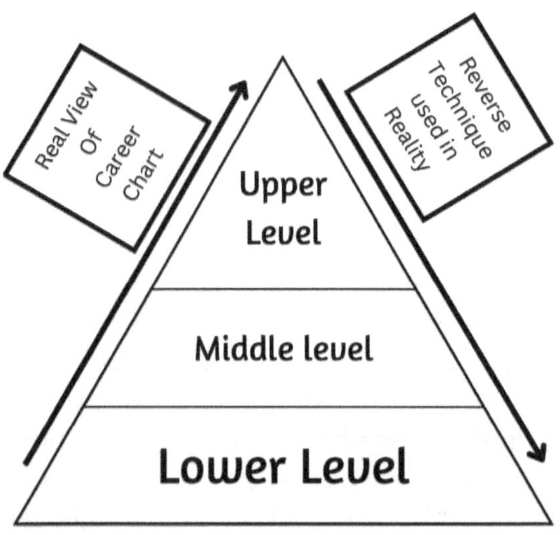

In this diagram, I have differentiated each level into different sizes. Let's just learn easily concepts to make it smooth for the decision as per your perspective clearance.

(Lower Level)

We all learned that we must start a career from zero to reach up in career positions. So, we may come across terms as workers, executive, billing desk, cashier, officer, teachers, peons, interns, etc. titles that don't matter. But I should appreciate them first because they are roots for the next levels. From tip to top their efforts are always measured first to complete any surveys.

I have specifically highlighted it in a bigger size so, that it's much easier to know the value.

(Middle Level)

We all know if we work somewhere then our skills should be trained and supervised. So, here comes our helpers who will help us reach top levels. Here we come across terms such as Supervisor, TL, Managers, Seniors, Project Head, Master, HR, etc. titles that don't matter. But I will give a big applause for them who exactly create diamonds. They are real goldsmith who makes ornaments ready for sale in any career (its example).

(Upper Level)

We all know the hot seat place is always shining to be at the top place. So, here comes our good ambassador who owns the pain with a title of a company which includes terms like CEO, VP, Chairman, Director, etc. They are owners of any commercials that make others earn and balance livelihood. Like a father is main to own a roof to safeguard a family and that's a reason we called it Mayor. Hence, a big thanks to this position who has borne each shoe's comfort to hide the journey efforts. We all wanted a good end before we start so, this is not an easy place believe it. Efforts matter to run from this top to make it run smoothly.

CHAPTER TWO

From Authors Desk

- **Sabita Dakua**

- **Qualification- BCom (BBI), PGDM in Business Administration, Content writer, Author of Books, and Psychology student**
- **Job Role-** Administration + Writer
- **My aim in life is- Spread happiness in the world and remove negativity in my surrounding.**
- **Job satisfaction (Happy/Unhappy)-** Happy as a writer but unhappy in the job.
- **Message to Youth-** A career is not one day journey. Be wise with whatever path you choose and always observe your skills are valued in terms of finance. In today's world if you want to live with your dreams then earning is the only source to reach your aim. Be sure that any manipulations are not done with your career as it may ruin your life and may make you negative in your path. Do remember one thing only education is not the source of income so, if you have some different passion, you can still survive happily. Always try to help the needy and move positively in life as success is part of failure first. Be a loser to win a big battle and fight back. Life

motivates you only if you know to get victory over your fear, depression, stress, mental and physical health.

"Career is not what you look for?
Career is what you work for."
"Learn to get the knowledge you work for
Learn to get paid what you struggle for"
"Never share your feedback negative to beginner
Never share the conclusion with the beginner"
"You can earn a degree but not attitude to disrespect anyone"

Interviews of different personalities-

CHAPTER THREE

Sunil Thakur

- **Qualification- MBA Marketing**
- **Job Role-** Area Director
- **My aim in life-** To reach my potential and to do good for myself and society.
- **Job satisfaction (Happy/Unhappy) –** Happy
- **Message to Youth-** Work hard for your dreams. Don't take shortcuts in life. Own your work with discipline about your aims and goals in life. To be a helping hand to everyone in bad times. Money matters in life so keep

working for it and make a career.

Email id - sunilkumarthakur@gmail.com

• 12 •

CHAPTER FOUR

Conclusion-

We came across almost the roles of careers with the help of interviews. As per our case study, we can observe with almost person thought that the below thing is necessary for life-

1. **Money**
2. **Skills**
3. **Positive attitude**
4. **Respect**
5. **Discipline**
6. **Aim**
7. **Dedication**
8. **Knowledge**
9. **Acceptance of any career**
10. **Winning battle**
11. **Education**
12. **Self-happiness**

Every person has come through different circumstances in life and still has not given up. They all fight for today's journey and are still focused on tomorrow's challenges. Everyone has not decided on the same aim in life but they survived with some or other

career paths. It is not necessary to be tagged as skilled and unskilled for work. There are still many options through which you can keep your passion and make it as a career but make sure to give your time 100% and gain knowledge.

Every entrepreneur or businessman doesn't need only a crore of money to set up some work with unique ideas. So, if you want something different in life follow the below paths-

1. Knowledge
2. Research
3. Capital
4. Good network
5. Market knowledge
6. Advertising
7. Skills improvement

So, whatever field you choose make sure you are comfortable with your work. Accept challenges as everyone is growing the same way. No one is blessed with a superpower without hard work and dreams. Make an oath to improve yourself and take a wise step for your career.

Hope this helps to clear doubts about choosing a career and make you confident to be happy always for your own decision. All the best for your bright future!!

CHAPTER FIVE

Meena Valecha

- **Qualification- MBA**
- **Job Role-** Admin Support
- **The aim in life-** Add value to the life of others.
- **Job satisfaction (Happy/Unhappy) –** Happy
- **Message to Youth-** While choosing your career listen to your instinct and follow your passion and see what your forte is. Choose your career in the field wherein you feel happy and contended and not what others say you to do. But yes, a career should give you money to survive. Skill

development is very important other than pure bookish knowledge.

Email id - meenavalechaa@gmail.com

CHAPTER SIX

Rajan Salvi

- **Qualification-** Graduation
- **Job Role-** Senior Process Associate
- **My aim in life-** Is to fulfill my parent's goals

To be happy without money

- **Job satisfaction (Happy/Unhappy)** -Unhappy
- **Message to Youth-** Try to do great things for our country India. Focus on your goals, not on your past.
- Email id - Rajan.skiller@gmail.com

CHAPTER SEVEN

Ali Rizvi

- **Qualification- Post Graduate**
- **Job Role-** Regional Head Sales
- **My aim in life-** To start my Footwear Manufacturing Unit.
- **Job satisfaction (Happy/Unhappy)** - Happy
- **Message to Youth-** Keep working to fulfill your dream after your family.
- Instagram Id- _money_matters_
- Email id- rizvialimurtuza@gmail.com

CHAPTER EIGHT

Ajay Sawant

- **Qualification- Graduate BCom**
- **Job Role-** Senior Process Analyst
- **My aim in life-** To make my mom happy
- **Job satisfaction (Happy/Unhappy)** -Unhappy
- **Message to Youth-** Keep Believe in yourself
- Email id – asajaycom686@gmail.com
- Instagram Id- _musaafir _hoon_yaaron_

CHAPTER NINE

Rajesh Chaudhary

- **Qualification-** LL.M.
- **Job Role-** Advocate
- **The aim in life-** Writer
- **Job satisfaction (Happy/Unhappy)** -Happy
- **Message to Youth-** Have faith in yourself and move ahead in life with your aim to reach your goal. World rule is to disturb you in mid-way by pointing out.
- Email id -rajeshchoudhary.5432@gmail.com

CHAPTER TEN

Vikrant Pawar

- **Qualification- Graduate BBI**
- **Job Role-** Senior Associate
- **The aim in life-** To be successful and achieve the goal which is a dream.
- **Job satisfaction (Happy/Unhappy) -** Happy
- **Message to Youth-** Pursue Your Passion When Choosing a Career.
- Email id – p.vikrant1512@gmail.com

CHAPTER ELEVEN

Dr. Rupali Wankhede

- **Qualification- B.A.M.S**
- **Job Role-** Doctor
- **The aim in life-** To help needy
- **Job satisfaction (Happy/Unhappy) –** Happy

- **Message to Youth-** Be yourself, recognize the skill in which you are the best and choose your Career wisely. Don't get under pressure from others about what they would feel if you chose some different career option. Focus on what you want to be. Give your 100 percent and success will be with you always. Once you reach your success goal, try to be humble and Kind then you will never be disappointed in Life.
- Email id - dr.rupali2010@gmail.com
- Insta ID- Rupali Wankhede (rups_ayurveda)

CHAPTER TWELVE

Mahesh N

- **Qualification-** Graduate + PGDM
- **Job Role-** Mechanical Engineer/Ops Mgt
- **The aim in life-** To contribute to ease the lives of society to make the world a better place for everyone.
- **Job satisfaction (Happy/Unhappy)-**

I'm satisfied with the opportunity to service

- **Message to Youth-** As a youth, you need to be active, alert & aware to do good deeds by having practical & optimistic patience.

- Email: maheshnasre15@gmail.com
- Instagram ID-mahesh_nasre

CHAPTER THIRTEEN

Yogendra Rawat

- **Qualification- Bachelor of Production Engineering**
- **Job Role-** Business Analyst
- **The aim in life-** To gain knowledge in any field the opportunity comes.
- **Job satisfaction (Happy/Unhappy) -**

Not yet and no one gets satisfied with the job when money matter comes.

- **Message to Youth**- Stay positive and move ahead with the present condition in life.
- Email id - yogendra.rawat2925@gmail.com
- Instagram Id- rawat.yogi

CHAPTER FOURTEEN

Rupali Kokate

- **Qualification-** Bachelor of science in microbiology. Diploma in the pathology lab. Certified reiki healer. The first exam cleared in classical singing.
- **Job Role-** Working in a government hospital pathology lab is challenging itself, with Emergency duties and Workload. We must handle every type of patient. It was highly challenging during a covid epidemic. I think that it's challenging but it satisfies me when patients get

cured. Other than this I had started a career as a vocalist so, I always make sure that both my roles I should have managed properly. Sometimes it's a bit challenging but when you must reach somewhere you automatically accept every challenge to reaching your goal.

- **The aim in life-** I was born in a typical middle-class family in the city of Amravati, but even though I come from a small place that didn't limit me to having higher goals/aims in life. I always believed we all get one life, so aim higher, even if we fail short, what better way is there to live chasing it? Aiming for financial freedom by building a career in singing as a playback singer. My mother wants to see me as a successful person in every aspect.

- **Job satisfaction (Happy/Unhappy)**

Currently I am working in this Kalyan Dombivli government hospital as a pathologist. As well as I'm recently active in a singing profession. I always wanted to be a successful artist and my dad wanted me to be a doctor. So, handling both sides happy. Because I like what I do, it makes my day-to-day challenges a bit easier. Every day is not the same, so choose what you love doing, even though it's a small thing do it by heart.

- **Message to Youth-** Our life is valuable, and it doesn't last forever, it is precious because it ends. Make your life count for something, and fight for what matters to you. Always put your honest effort into every work. Don't go for comfort zones, challenge yourself. Be positive. Remember, it's always fun to chase and do impossible Things. For me impossible means I-M-possible and I believe it.

- Email id - rupali14kokate@gmail.com
- Instagram Id- Rup_shakti/ Cleanest_aura_rups

CHAPTER FIFTEEN

Akshay Kamat

- **Qualification-** Post Graduation
- **Job Role-** HR
- **The aim in life-** Built something own.
- **Job satisfaction (Happy/Unhappy)** – Happy
- **Message to Youth-** Don't think much, time flies so have faith and do it.
- Email id - akshayark21@gmail.com
- Instagram Id- akshayark21

Sandeep Parashar

- **Qualification- B.E.**
- **Job Role-** Manager
- **The aim in life is-** Live happy and peaceful life.
- **Job satisfaction (Happy/Unhappy) –** Unhappy
- **Message to Youth-** To have rigor in the work that you do, only money minting should not be the aim.
- Email id - sandeep123parashar@gmail.com

Raviraj

- **Qualification- BCom**
- **Job Role-** Owner/ Proprietor
- **The aim in life is-** Live happily.
- **Job satisfaction (Happy/Unhappy) –** Happy
- **Message to Youth-** Live and Let Live.
- Email id - ravirajbkhairnar5487@gmail.com

Pawan

- **Qualification- BSc HMCTT**
- **Job Role-** Facility manager
- **The aim in life is-** Become a bright future.
- **Job satisfaction (Happy/Unhappy)** - So far so good
- **Message to Youth-** Born to lead@

Nothing is the impossible will to heart
Email id - pawanworld329@gmail.com

Bharat Salunkhe

- **Qualification-** SSC
- **Job Role-** Facility services
- **My aim in life-** Good Businessman.
- **Job satisfaction (Happy/Unhappy)** -Happy
- **Message to Youth-** I have not completed my education but I always dream to do new things in business. I feel this is a path where no specific qualification is required for startups if you have good ideas. I will always suggest learning in life and planning of second alternative ready

so that any bad situation would not affect the current source of income.

- Email id - bharatsalunkhe05@gmail.com
- Instagram Id- salunkhebharat8

CHAPTER TWENTY

Shankar Pawar

- **Qualification-** 5th STD
- **Job Role-** Painter
- **The aim in life-** To get stable life so that it never makes a condition to lean down.
- **Job satisfaction (Happy/Unhappy)-** Happy
- **Message to Youth-** Career can be made without education difference is illiterate put more effort and the

literate put less into doing hard work. But they both can earn in life. Knowledge should be there so education is important in today's changing world.

- Email id - shankarpawar44691@gmail.com

CHAPTER TWENTY-ONE

Sanjay Latkar

- **Qualification-** MVSc, MBA, PJDJMC
- **Job Role-** Trainer
- **My aim in life is-** Successful person in my job profile.
- **Job satisfaction (Happy/Unhappy) –** Happy
- **Message to Youth-** Choose your Career which you like and love
- Email id - drsanjayklat@gmail.com

Vignesh Kumar

- **Qualification-** B. Tech Chemical Engineer
- **Job Role-** Senior Executive in R&D
- **My aim in life-** To become the best writer and to be an entertainer.
- **Job satisfaction (Happy/Unhappy)** - Very much satisfied
- **Message to Youth-** Love yourself and do what you love.
- **Email id** - sdvigneshkumar12@gmail.com

- **Instagram Id-** withvicky12

San Jeeva

- **Qualification- B. Tech Civil Engineer**
- **Job Role-** Senior Quantity Surveyor (Construction)
- **The aim in life-** To become a successful Quantity Surveyor.
- **Job satisfaction (Happy/Unhappy)** -Partially Satisfied
- **Message to Youth-** Never forget to learn.

Subrat Das

- **Qualification-** B. Tech Environmental Engineer
- **Job Role-** Senior Environmental Consultant to Mumbai Rail Vikas Nigam
- **My aim in life is-** Give happiness to my parents.
- **Job satisfaction (Happy/Unhappy)-** A job can never be satisfactory.
- **Message to Youth-** Be sustainable as Earth is degrading.

CHAPTER TWENTY-FIVE

Deepak Kumar

- **Qualification- BCom**
- **Job Role-** Payment Analyst
- **The aim in life-** Manager
- **Job satisfaction (Happy/Unhappy)-** Good salary + Great Team.
- **Message to Youth-** If you have capabilities, opportunities are always there.
- Email id - deepakkumarc1994@gmail.com

Instagram Id- deepakkumar7936

CHAPTER TWENTY-SIX

Rohit Katam

- **Qualification-** MCom
- **Job Role-** Entrepreneur/ Head Coach
- **My aim in life-** To be the best coach, and mentor, and to create future stars in the badminton field.
- **Job satisfaction (Happy/Unhappy)-** As a player, I was never satisfied due to the lack of facilities. After starting

my academy and the facilities given to current kids for their betterment, I felt satisfaction. It is not just this but also the results matter for me as a job what I can do best for them.

- **Message to Youth-** DONT LOSE HOPE, NEVER EVER GIVE UP ON SHORT TERM FAILURE. Hope is the reason which gives us the reason to motivate ourselves and to keep fighting and moving forward. Failure is the 1st step to success so learn from every failure they are the life lessons for success which is waiting for you in the coming time.
- Email id - rohit.katam38@gmail.com
- Instagram Id- rohitkatam/ rkbadmintonacademy

CHAPTER TWENTY-SEVEN

Sadiya Boga

- **Qualification- BCom, MCom, TEFL, B.Ed student**
- **Job Role-** Academic Coordinator and Supervisor
- **The aim in life-** To educate as many as possible.
- **Job satisfaction (Happy/Unhappy)-** Highly privileged to work in an organization that provides light of education for a better future.
- **Message to Youth-** The world can be anything you want so, seek the best that you want yourself in.
- Email id – sidzuboga123@gmail.com

CHAPTER TWENTY-EIGHT

Rangeesh Chandrasekar

- **Qualification-** BCom, MBA in Finance, Diploma in Computer Applications (Tally Prime)
- **Job Role-** Employee at Infosys BPM- Bangalore
- **The aim in life-** To lead a simple life with stress-free & happy moments.

- **Job satisfaction (Happy/Unhappy)**- "Choose a job you love, and you'll never have to work a day in your life. It's not what you achieve, it's what you overcome. That's what defines your career."
- **Message to Youth**- *ADULT* has 5 letters, so does *YOUTH*

PERMANENT has 9 letters, so does *TEMPORARY*

GOOD has 4 letters, so does *EVIL*

BLACK has 5 letters, so does *WHITE*

CHURCH has 6 letters, so does *MOSQUE*

BIBLE has 5 letters, so does *QURAN*

LIFE has 4 letters, so does *DEAD*

HATE has 4 letters, so does *LOVE*

ENEMIES has 7 letters, and so does *FRIENDS*

LYING has 5 letters, so does *TRUTH*

HURT has 4 letters, so does *HEAL*

NEGATIVE has 8 letters, so does *POSITIVE*

FAILURE has 7 letters, so does *SUCCESS*

BELOW has 5 letters, so does *ABOVE*

CRY has 3 letters, so does *JOY*

ANGER has 5 letters, so does *HAPPY*

RIGHT has 5 letters, so does *WRONG*

RICH has 4 letters, so does *POOR*

FAIL has 4 letters, so does *PASS*

KNOWLEDGE has 9 letters, so does *IGNORANCE*

Are they all by Coincidence?

This means *LIFE* is like a double-edged sword but *the choice we make determines our future*

- Email id - rangeeshc1996@gmail.com
- Instagram Id- rangeeshc_1410

CHAPTER TWENTY-NINE

Akshay Jadhav

- **Qualification-** SSC
- **Job Role-** Supervisor at courier service
- **The aim in life is-** Live with financial freedom in life.
- **Job satisfaction (Happy/Unhappy) –** Happy
- **Message to Youth-** Take the risk in your life. If you can win you can lead, if you lose you can guide.
- **Email id-**aksh5514@gmail.com

Pratik

- **Qualification- BCom**
- **Job Role-** Auditor
- **The aim in life is-** Successful man.
- **Job satisfaction (Happy/Unhappy)** – When get appreciation from senior about my work.
- **Message to Youth-** Give your 100% whatever work you do

Supriya Gadekar

- **Qualification- Graduation**
- **Job Role-** Teacher
- **The aim in life is-** Teaching.
- **Job satisfaction (Happy/Unhappy) -** Happy
- **Message to Youth-** Education is most important in life for ladies.

Vineet Kumar

- **Qualification- B.E. MECHATRONICS**
- **Job Role-** Senior software engineer
- **The aim in life-** Startup
- **Job satisfaction (Happy/Unhappy) -** Happy
- **Message to Youth-** Work until you no longer must introduce yourself.
- Email id - vnthkumar12@gmail.com

CHAPTER THIRTY-THREE

Pranit Xavier

- **Qualification- Graduate BBI**
- **Job Role-** Entrepreneur
- **The aim in life-** Make your name so much that you don't need your introduction.
- **Job satisfaction (Happy/Unhappy)** – Happy
- **Message to Youth-** Follow your passion follow your dreams let that success come to you from miles.

Muralidhar Bansal

- **Qualification-** CA Inter, CS Foundation
- **Job Role-** Businessman
- **My aim in life is-** Positive businessman.
- **Job satisfaction (Happy/Unhappy)** - Happy
- **Message to Youth-** Avoid smoking and engage in social activities.

Shivam Singh

- **Qualification-** HSC Science
- **Job Role-** Businessman
- **The aim in life-** To obtain The Liberation till Eternity after this life.
- **Job satisfaction (Happy/Unhappy)** – Happy
- **Message to Youth-** "Have some curiosity to know about ourselves. Who are we? Just a body (which is always in continuous degradation) or are we a soul (which is Eternal)."

Ramu Gupta

- **Qualification- BCom**
- **Job Role-** Financial analyst
- **My aim in life-** To become Entrepreneur.
- **Job satisfaction (Happy/Unhappy) –** Happy
- **Message to Youth-** Enjoy your life and make life better with a smile.

Subasish Behera

- **Qualification- B. Tech Mechanical Engineer**
- **Job Role-** Manager in Supply Chain
- **The aim in life-** Head of Supply Chain.
- **Job satisfaction (Happy/Unhappy) - Happy**
- **Message to Youth-** Discipline with a daily task sheet helps in job life.
- Email Id- s.asish4u@gmail.com

CHAPTER THIRTY-EIGHT

Amit Mahadik

- **Qualification- BE Chemical Engineering**
- **Job Role-** Manager
- **My aim in life-** Live and enjoy stress free life.
- **Job satisfaction (Happy/Unhappy)-** Satisfied.
- **Message to Youth-** Build your expertise and enjoy with whatever you do. Education is a medium to skills. Focus on living life with enjoyment and don't just run behind money and career perspective. Don't carry regrets in life. You should have justified cause in life which is not limited to you. "Thoughts and words spoken should be upfront same to convey a concept than they will crack interview."

CHAPTER THIRTY-NINE

Hari Kumar Munjala

- **Qualification-** MS Computer Science, BTech EC and Red Hat certified
- **Job Role-** Senior Solution Engineer
- **My aim in life-** To setup product-based company.
- **Job satisfaction (Happy/Unhappy)-** Happy with job but goals are different so unhappy in that point of view.
- **Message to Youth-** Financial independence than you can do anything at that right time. Skill is important for a growth in life and Education is second factor but if you do job than its necessary for your career.

To The Readers

Shades of Career book is guidance book related to career confusions. Here we connect with different people stories and their progress in life. Some are truly inspiring and few are teaching us lessons that should not be repeated. Every person is wise in thoughts so, they think before doing anything in life. Career is a small word but changes anyone's life. It's a stage necessary in life to understand importance of life. There are many circumstances which may change our perceptions that doesn't mean we should cut roads and jump ahead in life. Our knowledge includes many things that doesn't mean all will club in one career some may change. After all career is always a crucial turn in everyone life and it has to be taken wisely.

Hope this clubbing of stories refresh your mind and convince self to be best always in each stage of knowledge to decide a better future ahead.

Thanks for reading!!!!
*©®Words_clubbed_*
-written by Sabita Dakua